ORDERING POSTERS

You can order attractive full-color posters to publicize your local production of this play. All posters are 11" x 17", full color, and include a large white space at the bottom for you to print personalized details, such as date, time, place, ticket prices, and contact information.

Prices below include shipping and handling, and are good through December 31, 2014. Please inquire about updated pricing after that date.

Poster Quantity	Total price	Poster Quantity	Total price
1	$6.00	100	$50.00
25	$20.00	150	$65.00
50	$30.00	200	$80.00
75	$40.00	250	$95.00

Orders ship within 24 hours of receipt. Anticipate 7–14 days for delivery. Please inquire for special handling or rush delivery.

TO ORDER ONLINE   Use code: POSTERS at www.principlesandchoices.com

TO ORDER BY PHONE*   Call: 425.481.6563

TO ORDER BY MAIL*   Send check to:
Healing the Culture
P.O. Box 82842
Kenmore, WA 98028

*Contact information may change. To verify phone and address, check contact page at **www.principlesandchoices.com**.

CHOOSING ANDREW

ROBERT & EMMA Act 1

Camille Pauley

with Chris Corey

CHOOSING ANDREW

ROBERT & EMMA *Act 1*

CAST

TEACHER: could be a man or a woman, 25–55

EMMA: fun, bright, attractive, strong voice and presence, 15–16

ROBERT: smart but lazy, not bad looking, wants to appear cool, 15–16

ANDREW ROSS: teenager with high-functioning Down Syndrome, happy, confident, 15-16

MARK: rough, obnoxious, rude, 15–16

CARL: Mark's sidekick, looking for trouble, 15–16

RECEPTIONIST: 35–60

JOEL ROSS: kind, compassionate, regular guy, 24–26

MRS. ROSS: late 40s, early 50s

STUDENT 1: 15–16

STUDENT 2: 15–16

ANONYMOUS AUDIENCE MEMBER: 15–16

TOTAL: 5 to 10 males and 2 to 7 females

This script contains the first act of a four-act play, designed for the high school classroom. The acts are divided into four separate books which correspond with a four-year curriculum entitled *Principles and Choices*©. The play may be produced as a full-length play by putting all four acts together. **To acquire Acts 2, 3, and 4, contact the publisher.**

There is little to no direction for sets, staging, and lighting. This act has no intermission, but if combined with Acts 2, 3, and 4 for a full-length play, an intermission can be placed between the second and third acts.

See copyright page for performance responsibilities and restrictions.

Act 1   CHOOSING ANDREW
ROBERT & EMMA

SCENE 1

(High school classroom, debate class. The students have chosen a partner and the teacher walks around handing each team a note card with writing on it.)

TEACHER: In two weeks, you and your partner will be debating in front of the entire student body *and* your parents. It'll be like a political debate where the audience will ask you questions, and each of you will have a chance to respond. You've got until the bell rings to decide who will argue for and against the topic, and to discuss how you will research your topic.

(Robert and Emma are paired together. Robert does not hide his boredom with the class, Emma can hardly wait to discover their topic.)

TEACHER: Go ahead and look at your cards.

(Emma flips their card over and reads it. The excitement on her face fades.)

EMMA: *(groans)* Should abortion be legal?

ROBERT: You're kidding me. Abortion? Couldn't we get something like gun control or global warming? Geez. *(sighing)* Well, obviously, I'm taking the pro-choice side.

EMMA: No... wait a minute!

ROBERT: Oh, c'mon Emma. As an "every-Sunday church girl," you're automatically pro-life...

EMMA: I don't know anything about abortion. Like... how do you argue it?

ROBERT: *(with a little sarcasm)* I don't know. Just say it's a baby.

EMMA: *(pointing toward the other students)* Look, they're all flipping coins. Let's do that.

ROBERT: I don't have a coin. You?

EMMA: No. Rock, paper, scissors?

> *(Robert rolls his eyes. Holds out his fist over his palm. Emma does the same.)*

ROBERT & EMMA: Rock, paper, scissors.

> *(Emma chooses rock, Robert chooses scissors.)*

ROBERT: You win, you choose.

EMMA: I'll take pro-life.

ROBERT: For real?

EMMA: What? You want pro-life?

ROBERT: No, but we just wasted time arguing about it when I already knew what you were gonna choose.

EMMA: Okay, sorry. So now what do we do.

ROBERT: I told you. Just do what all Christians do. Say it's a baby. We don't need two weeks. Here, look, let's practice.

EMMA: Okay.

ROBERT: *(puffs up his chest)* So, let's say you're pregnant and the law says you can't have an abortion. How will you finish high school young lady?

EMMA: *(mockingly triumphant)* It's a baby.

(Robert and Emma laugh.)

ROBERT: What if the pregnant mother is poor, has fifty-gazillion kids, no husband to support her, and they have to drink boiled sock water to survive?

EMMA: It's a baby. It can drink sock-water too...and...that's gross.

ROBERT: What if mom can't afford a bottle to put the sock-water in?

EMMA: Okay, now you're just being stupid.

ROBERT: What if it's deformed, or is gonna be born with some weird disability — like it's gonna be a total retard or something?

EMMA: You're a total retard, so you should be aborted. *(they burst out laughing)*

(Andrew, a student with Down Syndrome, has been listening to their conversation as he works with his partner. He frowns at their last exchange and then turns to them.)

ANDREW: Hey... um. Hey, Emma? *(looking at her and wincing)* That's not funny.

EMMA: Oh — hey, Andrew. We're just joking around.

ANDREW: I know. But that's not funny. I have Down Syndrome.

EMMA: I know, Andrew. That's okay.

ANDREW: No. Robert... Robert just said. *(pause)* He just said I should be aborted.

ROBERT: We didn't say that...

ANDREW: Yes you did. You said, "What if that baby is retarded and deformed and it should be aborted."

ROBERT: I wasn't talking about you, Andrew. I'm sorry if you took it that way. I didn't mean to get personal.

ANDREW: Did you know that my mom knew — before I was born... my mom knew that I had Down Syndrome?

EMMA: *(staring at Andrew)* Your mom knew?

ANDREW: *(excited)* Yeah. My mom knew. And all her friends said that she should abort me. Even the doctor said she should abort me. But my mom said, "No way."

ROBERT: I'm really glad your mom didn't abort you, Andrew. But this isn't about you. We're supposed to debate abortion. Not everyone's like your mom.

ANDREW: They could be if they wanted to.

ROBERT: Okay, that's cool. So... can we get back to work now?

EMMA: Shut up, Robert. *(turns to Andrew.)* Andrew, can I ask you something?

ANDREW: Sure, Emma. You can ask me anything!

EMMA: So, like, don't take me the wrong way or anything — I totally don't want to hurt your feelings. But most mother's choose to get rid of their baby when they find out it has a disability. Why didn't your mom?

ANDREW: Because my mom loves me!

ROBERT: Yeah, but most people don't want a disabled kid if they had the choice. That's why doctors do tests. So parents can have a choice.

ANDREW: I don't know why they would care. I'm a great kid.

ROBERT: I know that, but some parents don't want, or can't take care of a disabled kid.

ANDREW: Why not?

ROBERT: I don't know. Maybe it's too hard. 'Cause they know the kid won't have a normal, happy life.

ANDREW: Well, maybe you should ask the kid if he thinks he can be happy before you abort him.

ROBERT: He wouldn't even know what happiness is.

ANDREW: I'm happy!

ROBERT: Yeah, but Andrew, you're not as disabled as a lot of other kids are.

ANDREW: So?

EMMA: So, you can do a lot of things other kids can't.

ANDREW: Like what?

ROBERT: Like, walking, eating... you can talk... you can think...

ANDREW: But that's not what makes me happy.

EMMA: What makes you happy?

ANDREW: *(yells)* My mom loves me!

   (Emma laughs.)

ROBERT: *(smirking)* That's it? That's all that makes you happy?

ANDREW: Well, you love me too, right Robert? And you love me too, right Emma?

ROBERT: Yeah, but Andrew, some kids have it really hard. I mean, some are in wheelchairs, or can't do things on their own. They don't have a chance to have a job, or have any kind of quality of life. They'll always need someone to take care of them. I don't think you should stop a parent from having an abortion when the kid might be really screwed up or might not even live after they're born.

ANDREW: Yeah... That's what they said about me. I was born with a heart defect. But I'm still alive!!! *(pumps the air)* **Yeah!!**

(Emma smiles while Robert looks around the room slightly embarrassed. The teacher comes over.)

TEACHER: Andrew, calm down. All three of you need to get back to work.

(Andrew hunches his shoulders a little, smiles at Robert and Emma, puts his finger to his lips and makes a "shh" sound. He walks away.)

(Robert and Emma go back to their discussion.)

ROBERT: That was an over-simplified view.

EMMA: What do you mean?

ROBERT: Look, I like Andrew okay and all, but, I mean, seriously? It isn't realistic for all parents to act like his mom did. Not everyone can have a perfectly happy life like he does.

EMMA: You think his life is perfect? He gets made fun of every day by people who totally don't even want to take the time to understand him.

ROBERT: Whatever.

EMMA: You always say that when I'm right.

(The bell rings. Robert and Emma start gathering their things.)

ROBERT: I hate this topic. Oh—you ready for the track meet tomorrow?

EMMA: We'll find out. Pretty sure the coach is gonna push me hard with state on the line.

ROBERT: You'll do fine. Meet me at eight-thirty before it starts and we'll warm up together.

EMMA: Cool.

SCENE 2

(The scene is set on the track field at school. Robert walks onto the field and joins two friends, Mark and Carl, who are already warming up. There's an ambulance on the field that's holding up the warm-up before the meet. Mark and Carl show their frustration at the delay.)

ROBERT: What happened? Is it someone from our team?

MARK: No, man. Freak-show Andrew was running around on the field like an idiot and collapsed.

CARL: Why they even let kids like that in school anyway? He's always walking around the hallway with his shoes untied, and dropping his books and all. He's like a total joke.

(Mark laughs. Robert just stretches.)

MARK: *(still laughing)* And when we laugh, he thinks we're laughing with him. He's clueless, man. It would be sad if it wasn't so funny!

CARL: Dude, I don't know why you're laughing. You're almost as big a klutz as he is.

MARK: You're comparing me to Drew-tard? Didn't he get a better grade then you in math class? He got like a "C-minus" and you got a... what?

> *(Carl says nothing.)*

MARK: *(continues)* What? I didn't hear that. Let's just ask my man Robert over here. What did Carl get in math?

ROBERT: Word on the street? Carl got a "D."

MARK: Carl got a "D." Drew-tard got a "C." And Carl got a... what?

ROBERT: I believe the letter you're looking for is "D."

MARK: Today's episode is brought to you by the letter –

ROBERT: "D"

CARL: Yeah, whatever.

MARK: Dude, why you even in the same math class as him?

CARL: I hate math.

ROBERT: I would too if I were you.

CARL: Shut up. We got a meet to get ready for anyway.

ROBERT: Oh, so now you want to get all serious.

MARK: Can't stand the heat?

CARL: Seriously. You're wrecking with my mood over here. *(looks in the direction of the ambulance)* Looks like the ambulance is getting ready to leave.

ROBERT: *(to Mark)* You serious? That was Andrew?

MARK: Bro, I'm tellin' ya. I saw it go down. The dude was chasing this dog around on the field and he was all making these barking sounds. I about died laughing.

CARL: Ambulance is leaving.

ROBERT: Finally. Maybe we'll still get a few minutes to warm up.

MARK: Maybe they'll start the meet late.

CARL: Doubt it. They never do that.

(Emma approaches. She looks visibly shaken, her arms folded as if she's cold. She tries to hold herself back from crying further and wipes her eyes to hide that she has been.)

ROBERT: What's up Emma? Why aren't you dressed for the meet?

EMMA: I'm not going to the meet. I'm going to the hospital.

ROBERT: You're missing the meet? Why?

EMMA: I'm going to see Andrew. They said he might have had a heart attack.

MARK: Figures.

EMMA: What's that supposed to mean?

MARK: Doesn't surprise me, that's all. Guys like him are always slowing the rest of us down.

CARL: What the man means is that slower kids like Andrew are always holding up class or getting hurt or ruining it for the rest of us normal people.

EMMA: Do you know what happened out there? You know why he got hurt?

MARK: Yeah, I saw him running around the field like a monkey on caffeine, barking and yelling and all.

EMMA: Is that all you saw?

MARK: Wasn't much else to see, man. He kinda took center stage.

EMMA: Really? So you didn't see the big dog on the field?

CARL: That's why he was barking! He was chasing a dog.

EMMA: Yeah. He was chasing a dog. But do you even know why?

MARK: Because that's what fools like Andrew do. Am I right, Robert?

(Mark holds up his fist for Robert to bump. Without thinking, Robert bumps it.)

EMMA: You're going to give that a bump? Really? You guys make me sick.

(Emma starts to walk away.)

ROBERT: Emma, wait. C'mon. You can't just forfeit.

EMMA: Right now, I couldn't care less about a stupid race, especially when there are teammates like you guys around.

(Emma starts to walk away. She pauses and turns back around.)

EMMA: That's *funny*... teammates. You know, when we compete, Andrew's always cheering for us louder than the whole cheer squad. I kinda thought it was annoying until I saw him here this morning when I was crossing the field. He was here before anyone else, putting out towels and setting up water for us to drink. He was serving the team. I didn't even think about it until I was crossing the field, and some gigantic stray dog started charging me. Without hesitating, Andrew started chasing the dog.

(Emma pauses, wipes a tear from her eye.)

EMMA: He wasn't barking for your amusement. He was barking to get the dog's attention. Next thing I know, the dog's gone and Andrew's on the field unconscious. I heard one of the paramedics say he probably had a heart attack. He's in an ambulance on the way to the hospital. Whatever you might think of him, Andrew was more of a teammate to me today than any of you guys have ever been.

ROBERT: So that's it? You're just going to blow off the meet? We do well today, we have a shot at state.

EMMA: Robert, these two jerks I get. But you? I thought you of all people would understand. I even thought you'd come with me.

ROBERT: C'mon Em. Just go after the meet. I'll go with you then.

EMMA: They think Andrew had a heart attack. If he did, it's because of me. And I'm really freaked out he's not going to be okay.

(Robert pauses as an awkward moment passes between he and Emma.)

EMMA: You really won't come with me?

ROBERT: Emma, there are supposed to be college scouts here. I'm not missing the meet.

EMMA: Fine. Hope you get a fantastic scholarship.

(Emma storms off. Robert wants to say something but fails to find the words.)

MARK: Awkward.

ROBERT: Shut up, Mark.

(Robert walks towards the field.)

SCENE 3

(Joel, a young man in his early twenties, sits in a hospital emergency room waiting area reading a magazine while the receptionist enters data into her computer. Emma bursts through the doors, a little out of breath, and rushes to the reception counter...)

EMMA: I got here as fast as I could.

RECEPTIONIST: I'm sorry...?

EMMA: I'm here to see a friend. I was told he was brought here. Is he okay? I heard he had a heart attack, or something like that — he's going to be alright, isn't he?

RECEPTIONIST: Miss, you need to slow down so I can understand you.

EMMA: My friend. He's supposed to be here.

RECEPTIONIST: Okay, let's start with a name.

EMMA: Emma, my name is Emma.

RECEPTIONIST: Nice to meet you, Emma. Now let's try the patient's name.

EMMA: Oh, right. Sorry. Ross. Andrew Ross. He passed out at school today.

RECEPTIONIST: *(typing in the name)* School, huh? You know today is Saturday, right?

EMMA: Right. It was at our track meet.

(Joel recognizes Emma and makes his way across the room to her.)

RECEPTIONIST: Well he's here. Are you part of the family?

EMMA: No, just a friend.

JOEL: *(Interrupting)* Hey, Emma. What are you doing here?

EMMA: Oh...hi. You're Andrew's brother, Joel, aren't you? I've seen you at our track meets.

JOEL: Right. Don't you have a meet right now?

EMMA: Yeah, but... Is Andrew okay?

JOEL: *(seeing that she is shaken)* You wanna wait with me over here and we can talk?

EMMA: Okay.

(They return to where Joel was waiting and they sit down.)

JOEL: All I heard was that he passed out. Mom called me, frantic, and said there was an emergency with Andrew. When I got here, they said he's gonna be alright. They're just running a few more tests.

EMMA: *(relieved)* Oh, good. I ran all the way here. The paramedics made it sound really serious.

JOEL: You ran? Wow. You're pretty fast.

EMMA: You come to a lot of our meets, don't you?

JOEL: As many as I can. Now that I'm out of college, I can go to more games and meets with Andrew. He really loves sports.

EMMA: I like that you and your mom and dad come to the meets, even though Andrew doesn't compete or anything.

JOEL: Being a part of the team's really important to him. Even if it's just cheering from the stands. So, were you there when it happened?

EMMA: Yeah. He kinda tried to save my life.

JOEL: He did?

EMMA: Yeah. I was walking across the track field to get to the locker rooms and this big dog came out of nowhere and rushed me. Next thing I know, Andrew's chasing the dog, barking at it to get it away from me. I started running from the dog and when I looked back, Andrew was lying on the field. I ran and got help and...

JOEL: That sounds like Andrew. He shouldn't be running like that, though. It was probably the stress from running that caused him to pass out.

EMMA: I know I couldn't do anything, but I feel like this is my fault somehow.

JOEL: Andrew's had a heart defect since he was born. It's pretty common for someone with Down Syndrome. They corrected it with surgery, but he had some complications and he's supposed to be really careful.

EMMA: Then why would he do that? If he knows he could get hurt...

JOEL: That's just who he is. I mean, the kid's got a heart of gold. He doesn't think twice about putting someone else's needs before his own. He probably would have kicked that dog's butt... if he hadn't passed out first.

EMMA: Do you think he could have died?

JOEL: Maybe. But Andrew doesn't think like that. He's always thinking of other people. I guess that's what makes him such a happy guy.

EMMA: Yeah, he is pretty happy. I mean, jerks at school are always making fun of him and giving him a hard time. But he doesn't let it bother him. I think it's awful that he has Down Syndrome when he's such a good person. It's not fair.

JOEL: You know, I used to feel that way. I was actually ticked off about it. We found out Andrew had Down Syndrome when my mom was pregnant. When I heard I wasn't gonna have a normal brother...I told my mom... *(trails off)*

EMMA: What?

JOEL: Well, honestly, I told her she should have an abortion.

EMMA: You did?

JOEL: *(nods)* Yeah. A lot of people did. I thought my parents should just hit the reset button and try for a kid that would be normal. I can't believe I'm telling you this...

EMMA: I'm sorry. I don't mean to...

JOEL: Nah, it's cool. I was a jerk. I didn't want anything to do with Andrew at first. When he was a baby, I saw all the special things my parents had to do to try and keep him healthy. All the hospital trips. The surgeries. The way they had to care for him. They didn't have as much time for me. I resented them and I resented Andrew.

(Emma pauses and lets Joel gather his thoughts.)

JOEL: Then one day, when he was finally able to walk on his own, he just walked up to me and hugged me. He held onto me and wouldn't let go. It was weird, but suddenly, I couldn't be mad at him anymore. All that anger at my parents, Andrew, and the whole thing didn't seem to matter anymore. Dad isn't so sure, but to this day, I swear I heard his first word in that moment. "Love." Mom said it was just baby babble, but I know what I heard.

EMMA: Wow.

JOEL: It's not like Andrew's special needs changed at all. But I was able to look at it differently. I mean, we all have special needs in some way. If you count how many times my parents took Andrew to the doctors or the hospital, and put it up against how many times they took me to football and baseball practices and games, five days a week for six months out of the year...they probably did at least as much for me as they did for Andrew. And it's not even about that, though. I mean, it just puts it in perspective.

EMMA: I always wondered about how Andrew thought about not being able to do things like sports or things other kids get to do.

JOEL: Well, like I said, Andrew doesn't think that way. Sure, he'd love to be on the field, even though he knows he can't. But that doesn't stop his heart from being on the field. When he was at my games, he was my biggest fan. I'd be on the field with the whole football stadium cheering like crazy, but I could always hear Andrew over them. And you know what? It made me play better. In a way, when we won a game, I always felt like he was as much a part of our win as the rest of the team.

EMMA: A lot of people look at Andrew as a burden. I mean, even one of my friends said that he slows the rest of us down. I told Andrew a few days ago that most mom's who find out their kid's gonna be born like that would abort it. When I said it, I wasn't even thinking about how Andrew might feel. But he didn't get offended.

JOEL: Andrew doesn't hold grudges, that's for sure. Thank goodness. He's always looking for who you are on the inside. He notices things about people that the rest of us don't see because we're too focused on the outside.

EMMA: That's so amazing. I mean, if somebody said something rude to me, I would *not* feel like putting myself at risk to save them from a mad dog.

JOEL: I don't think love is about how you feel. I think it's about choosing to do what's good for someone else, even when you don't feel like it.

EMMA: That's what Andrew did for me today.

JOEL: Yep. And it's what my mom did for Andrew when she gave him life, even though everyone around her told her it was a mistake. It's what Andrew did for me when he hugged me, even though I resented him. I try to compare my choices to what Mom and Andrew do, and it makes me a better person. They're my heroes.

(Emma is about to say something when a pair of double-doors burst open. Andrew's mother and father wheel him out in a wheelchair. Andrew beams when he sees Emma.)

ANDREW: EMMA! Look at me! I got wheeeeels!

EMMA: That's great, Andrew. Looks like fun.

ANDREW: It was so cool, Joel. They had me all hooked up. I looked like a space robot.

JOEL: You rock! *(does a high-five with Andrew, and then turns to his mom)* What'd they say?

MRS. ROSS: He'll be okay, but the doctor wants to talk to us in the conference room.

(Joel talks quietly with his mom and dad.)

ANDREW: Emma... Are you going to come?

EMMA: Oh. No, I can't come with you, Andrew. I just wanted to make sure you're okay.

ANDREW: I never felt better. I hope they let me keep this wheelchair. Want to ride in it with me?

EMMA: *(chuckles a little)* No thanks, Andrew. Listen... I feel bad about what I said in class last week. And I feel bad that you got hurt on the field. I just wanted to say I'm sorry.

ANDREW: No way, Emma. You're my friend. I would've kicked that dog's butt.

(The doctor emerges and greets the family. They are brought into a conference room. Andrew waves to Emma as the door closes. Emma is left standing there, taking in what Andrew just said.)

SCENE 4

(The high school auditorium is filled with students and parents. Robert and Emma are standing next to each other on stage behind two podiums with microphones. There is a microphone on a floor stand next to the audience. Two students are lined up behind it. The teacher is between Robert and Emma on the stage getting ready to introduce them. Robert is casually leaning on his podium and smirking at the audience, giving the casual "I got this" nod to his friends. Emma looks focused and determined, with a knowing maturity we have not seen from her yet. She checks her notes and readies herself.)

TEACHER: Remember, we will be taking three questions from the audience. Our debaters will each have one minute to respond to the first two questions, and two minutes for the last question. Our final debaters for the evening will be Robert and Emma. The topic for their debate is: "Should abortion be legal?"

(The audience claps while the teacher takes a seat. When the applause dies down, the first question is raised.)

STUDENT 1: Okay, so, like, my question is that, um... every child should be wanted right? I mean, if you make abortion illegal, what are you gonna do with all those unwanted children? Doesn't abortion help solve that problem?

TEACHER: Emma?

EMMA: Of course every child should be wanted. But the fact that there are nearly 2 million couples in America waiting to adopt a baby means that there is no such thing as an unwanted baby. My opponent believes that if a child isn't wanted by her parents, it should be legal to kill her. I think that's cruel and unfair. Why should we make it legal to kill babies just because their parents don't want them? Think about it this way... If you knew that your next door neighbors were physically abusing their five-year-old daughter because they didn't love her, you wouldn't think to yourself, "Gosh, the government should really make it legal for those parents to kill their child so that she doesn't have to be unwanted." Most people would want to take that child away from her parents and try to find somebody who *would* love her. When parents don't want their own children, even when it's for good reasons like they can't afford another child, then it's up to the rest of us to stand up and say, "Don't kill your child. We want her. We'll take your child." Our country spends millions of dollars on abortion. What if, instead, we spent millions of dollars finding loving homes for the children whose parents don't want them?

TEACHER: Time! Robert, your response.

ROBERT: Okay, so Emma's my buddy and I think she's great and all... but she's not being very realistic. You can't legislate love. You gotta let people be free and decide for themselves how many kids they want. People should be able to get an abortion without the government getting all in your face. It's your life, man. It's your business. If you want to love your kids, great. If you don't, why should you be forced to have them? Emma acts like the parents have a problem if they don't want a kid because they won't love it. So what now? Emma's the "love police?" Is she gonna run around and force everybody to love their kids, and put them in jail if they don't? You can't force people to love each other, and you can't legislate family relationships. The government should stay out of the bedroom and let people think for themselves. Besides, a lot of people would rather abort their baby than give it up for adoption. Maybe that's cruel, but that's their choice. So what? It's a free country.

TEACHER: Time!

MARK: Nice one, bro!

CARL: You rock, Bobby-boy!

ANONYMOUS AUDIENCE MEMBER: *(sarcastically yelling)* I love you, Robert!

TEACHER: Next question, please.

STUDENT 2: So... You keep talking about the happiness of the child, but what about women? I think that a woman should have the right to have an abortion because she might want to go to college, or get a better job, or make a lot of money or something, and having a baby would get in her way. Shouldn't she have the right to pursue happiness?

TEACHER: Robert?

ROBERT: Absolutely right! If my opponent had her way, we'd all be living in a time when women were treated like servants to men and were second class citizens. I don't think any of us want to go back to that. Especially women...

EMMA: Hold on a minute...

TEACHER: Emma, Robert has the floor.

ROBERT: They weren't allowed to vote. They weren't allowed into a lot of jobs. They were discriminated against and weren't even allowed to make as much money as men. Legal abortion lets women follow their dreams and be whatever they want to be. If you make abortion illegal, you'll be closing the door on millions of women who will be pushed back into the kitchen, barefoot and pregnant. All you girls who wanna go to college? Forget it. Wanna be a doctor or a lawyer? Not a chance. If Emma has her way, it's game over, ladies. You want happiness in life, you gotta get a good job, make a lot of money, or at least be famous and not have to spend your whole life changing diapers and wiping snot off some kid's nose. Sure, that may be fine for Emma, but a lot of women have bigger dreams that don't include kids.

TEACHER: Time!

EMMA: Wait a minute... That's really sexist. Why should women have to kill their own babies to be able to stay in school or get a good job? Being a woman isn't a disease, Robert. Our ability to get pregnant and have children is part of what makes women so special. It's time for women to stop acting like we're supposed to be ashamed of our fertility, and start demanding that people like Robert respect our unique gifts while still giving us all the opportunities that men have. That means helping us pursue our dreams without making us feel like abortion is our only option if we get pregnant. Secondly, *Robert*, may think that happiness is all about money and success and not having any responsibilities to anyone but yourself; but I think most women can see right through that. It's not that I don't think those things are important. I'd like to be successful and make a lot of money too. I mean, who wouldn't? But not at the cost of another person's right to life. There's a lot more to happiness than just living for yourself.

ROBERT: *(mocking)* Like what?

> *(Emma is about to answer when the back doors of the auditorium open. She watches as Andrew, his mother, and Joel enter. The audience turns to see who Emma is looking at. The three take their seats and Emma answers Robert while looking at Andrew.)*

EMMA: Like self-sacrifice and love. Like generosity and compassion. Like making a difference to someone else who needs you and who depends on you. Like living your life for something bigger than yourself.

TEACHER: Time! Okay, last question. *(pause, noticing that there is no one at the microphone)* Does anyone else want to ask the debaters a question about abortion?

(Andrew rises from his seat and, with Joel at his side, they approach the microphone.)

ANDREW: *(with enough enthusiasm to make the microphone screech)* Hi Robert!

ROBERT: *(uneasy)* Hey, Andrew.

ANDREW: Wow, Emma, you look so pretty.

(Audience chuckles.)

EMMA: Thank you, Andrew.

TEACHER: Andrew, did you have a question?

(Andrew begins unfolding a piece of paper from his pocket.)

ANDREW: Yes. I wrote this myself. Joel helped a little. *(begins to read)* Hi. My name is Andrew. I have Down Syndrome. I also have a heart con... con...

JOEL: *(quietly, to help Andrew)* Condition.

ANDREW: Condition. Thanks Joel. I have a heart condition, so I can't do a lot of things. I can't do sports or join the marsh...ma... ma...

JOEL: Marching band.

ANDREW: Marching band. My grades aren't too good either. But none of those things really matter to me. You matter to me. And Emma and Robert and my brother and mom and dad and all my friends matter to me. I don't think you should—you shouldn't judge someone because they are han...han... *(whispers to Joel)* What's that one?

JOEL: Handicapped.

ANDREW: Han... handicapped. You should only judge people by what's in their hearts. And you can't know what's in their hearts if you kill them before they are even born.

TEACHER: That was very well stated, Andrew. Do you have a question for our debaters?

ANDREW: Yeah, but I'm not done yet.

TEACHER: I understand, Andrew, but we have limited time, and we need to give Robert and Emma time to respond to your question.

ROBERT: *(like he's scheming a way to get off easy)* He can have my time.

TEACHER: Oh. Well... okay. Go ahead Andrew. Robert has generously forfeited his time to you.

ANDREW: Thanks Robert! You're my friend!

(Robert looks a little embarrassed. Some of his friends snicker at him.)

ANDREW: Okay. So... *(Joel points to the spot on Andrew's paper where he left off)* Oh yeah. My mom loves me. She chose life for me. Some people say that other moms should be able to choose abortion if their baby is disabled like me. But what if my mom was somebody else and she wanted an abortion? Then I wouldn't be here. What about my choice?

(Andrew looks at Joel, who puts an arm around his shoulder. Andrew and Emma share a smile.)

TEACHER: Emma, you've got two minutes to close.

(She draws a deep breath, looks across the audience, and delivers her next lines calmly.)

EMMA: Andrew doesn't like it when we distinguish between him and the rest of us — as if he wasn't completely human or something. But I need to show you the difference between him and us, because maybe it's not Andrew that's missing something in life. Maybe it's the rest of us.

When was the last time you saw Andrew get angry or hurt somebody? Have you ever seen him cheat on a test, take something that didn't belong to him, or even say something mean about someone else? I'll bet the rest of us have all done these things. But I haven't seen Andrew do them. Maybe these things are the real disabilities in our world.

Ninety percent of all Down Syndrome children are aborted. That number is pretty consistent among all disabilities, not just Down Syndrome. How many Andrews are missing from our world because our law on abortion has taught us to believe that their disabilities are worse than ours? We've grown up in a culture that had legal abortion long before we were born. And it hasn't solved any of the problems that people say it's supposed to. There's still poverty in the world. There are still people with disabilities. And there are still people with no one to care for them.

But we're also growing up in a culture where kids like us have incredible opportunities to create new solutions to human problems. See, we do have a choice. We can choose a world where we continue to kill people with disabilities. Or we can change the world, and make it better for people like them. *(She looks at Andrew now.)* As for me, I think we need you Andrew. Without you, we may have a world full of choices, but it will be a very dark and selfish place to live. We need you more than we need doctors and lawyers, scientists, and engineers. Those people have important jobs. But people like you are the ones who lead the rest of us to love. And in case I haven't told you this, you're my friend, Andrew.

> *(Emma surveys the audience, which has fallen to an awkward silence. The hush in the auditorium seems to last forever...until, from the back of the room, the echoing sound of a student clapping cuts through the silence. After a moment, Joel begins to clap, slowly and loudly as he looks at Emma smiling.)*

> *(It isn't long before the entire auditorium is filled with the sound of applause. Joel puts his arm around Andrew, who is smiling ear to ear. Joel looks around and ups the ante...)*

JOEL: *(chanting)* **An-drew! An-drew! An-drew!...**

> *(Like the applause, the audience slowly begins to chant Andrew's name. Andrew looks around, completely overwhelmed at the cheers of his name. He looks back at Emma, who is unable to keep the emotions out of her eyes as she mouths: "Thank you, Andrew.")*